Documenting History

Documenting Women's Suffrage

Peter Hicks

rosen publishing's
rosen central®

New York

Published in 2010 by The Rosen Publishing Group Inc.
29 East 21st Street, New York, NY 10010

First Edition

Senior editor: Camilla Lloyd
Designer: Phipps Design
Consultant: Dr Paul Readman
Picture researcher: Shelley Noronha
Indexer and proofreader: Cath Senker

Library of Congress Cataloging-in-Publication Data

Hicks, Peter, 1952-
 Documenting women's suffrage / Peter Hicks. -- 1st ed.
    p. cm. -- (Documenting history)
 Includes bibliographical references and index.
 ISBN 978-1-4358-9672-7 (library binding)
 ISBN 978-1-4358-9675-8 (paperback)
 ISBN 978-1-4358-9680-2 (6-pack)
 1. Women--Suffrage--Great Britain--History--Juvenile literature. 2. Women--Suffrage--
United States--History--Juvenile literature. 3. Suffragists--Great Britain--History--
Juvenile literature. 4. Suffragists--United States--History--Juvenile literature.
 5. Women--Suffrage--Great Britain--History--Sources--Juvenile literature. 6. Women--
Suffrage--United States--History--Sources--Juvenile literature. I. Title.
 JN979.H53 2010
 324.6'230941--dc22
                                        2009026076

Photo Credits:
The author and publisher would like to thank the following for allowing their pictures to
be reproduced in this publication: Cover: Main: © Bettmann/ CORBIS, BL: Museum of
London / HIP / TopFoto; 1 Hulton Archive/Getty Images, 4 Rare Books& Special Collections
Division,Library of Congress, Washington, DC, 5 Hulton Archive/Getty Images, 6
Smithsonian National Postal Museum, 7 © Bettmann/CORBIS, 8 © Hulton-Deutsch
Collection/CORBIS, 9 The Print Collector / HIP /TopFoto, © Hulton-Deutsch Collection/ COR-
BIS, 11 Hulton Archive/Getty Images, 13 Mary Evans Picture Library,
14 Mary Evans Picture Library/ The Women's Library, 15 Hulton Archive/Getty Images.
17 Schlesinger Library, Radcliffe Institute, Harvard University/ The Bridgeman Art Library,
18 ©TopFoto, 19 Museum of London / HIP/TopFoto, 20 Mary Evans Picture Library, The
Women's Library, 21 Hulton Archive/Getty Images, 22 Museum of London / HIP / TopFoto,
23 Museum of London / HIP / TopFoto, 24 The Illustrated London News Picture Library,
London, U.K.,/The Bridgeman Art Library , 25 © Bettmann/CORBIS, 26 © Bettmann/COR-
BIS, 27 ©McNeely Image Services / The Image Works/Topfoto, 28 ©McNeely Image
Services / The Image Works/Topfoto, 29 Schlesinger Library, Radcliffe Institute, Harvard
University/ The Bridgeman Art Library, 30, 31 Topfoto, 32 Private Collection/ The
Bridgeman Art Library, 35 Topfoto, 36 Hulton Archive/Getty Images, 37 Wayland, 39 Hulton
Archive/Getty Images, 40, 41 © Bettmann/CORBIS, 42 Mary Evans Picture Library, 43
Museum of London / HIP / TopFoto, 44 Hulton Archive/Getty Images.

Manufactured in China
CPSIA Compliance Information: Batch #WAW0102YA: For Further Information
contact Rosen Publishing, New York, New York at 1-800-237-9932

CONTENTS

The suffrage movement begins

In the spring of 1866, a group of women from London, England, led by Barbara Bodichon, Emilia Boucherette, and Rosamund Hill, decided to organize a petition to present to Parliament. It was to be handed in by John Stuart Mill, the philosopher and radical Liberal MP (Member of Parliament). At the time, Parliament was debating a Reform Bill to increase the number of men who could vote. J. S. Mill, a fervent believer in women having and exercising the vote, agreed to introduce a women's suffrage amendment to the bill if the women organized the petition. This duly happened and on June 7, 1866, Mill presented the petition to Parliament with 1,499 women's signatures on it. It respectfully asked that as property was the basis for the right to vote, it was only fair that women who owned property should be able to vote. It is at this point that the women's suffrage movement in Britain properly began. Women who campaigned for the vote and tried to win public support for were known as "suffragists."

Barbara Bodichon and her friends were part of a tradition that believed women could contribute a great deal to society, but were held back by lack of opportunities in education, in the workplace, and in the political and legal world. These ideas had been voiced by Mary Wollstonecraft as early as 1792 in her book *A Vindication of the Rights of Women*.

A later publication that specifically mentioned the idea of votes for women was *Appeal of One Half of the Human*

SOURCE

BOOK

Mary Wollstonecraft did not actually mention the vote in *A Vindication of the Rights of Women*, but she did argue that because of women's lack of education and the chains of marriage, they were little better than slaves. She hated the fact women were expected to be beautiful but *"not to think."*

The great Chartist demonstration held on Kennington Common, south London, in April 1848. The plan was to march on Parliament with the People's Charter and a petition for electoral reform, which did not include women.

Race, written by the philosopher William Thompson and Anne Wheeler in 1825. It argued *"nothing could be more easy than to put the rights of women, political and civil, on a perfect equality with those of men."* These writings established strong arguments supporting the view that women's position in society would improve if they had a political voice.

During the 1830s and 1840s, a working-class movement called Chartism was formed. It focused on a People's Charter and its six points, one of which was universal suffrage—the vote for all irrespective of gender. Local Chartist groups had many women members, and when the Charter was planned, female suffrage was included. This was later dropped because the leadership feared it was such a revolutionary idea that the reform of men's suffrage would suffer.

In February 1851, the Sheffield Association for Female Franchise held its first meeting and asked: *"What is liberty, if the chains of women be disregarded?"* which echoed the poet Percy Bysshe Shelley's famous line *"Can man be free if woman be a slave!"* The group's aim was to ensure the vote for all women, but with no national organization for like-minded women to join, there was nowhere to channel their energies.

It was the failure to include women's right to the vote in the Second Reform Act, passed in 1867, that really spurred on women's groups. To win the vote, they would have to fight and campaign more effectively. Organization was essential, so in 1867, with Lydia Becker as national secretary, the National Society for Women's Suffrage (NSWS) was formed.

The sacred right to vote

It was events in Britain that inspired a group of American women to organize themselves and fight for equal rights with men. In 1840, Elizabeth Cady Stanton and Lucretia Mott, both Quakers (a Christian sect that believed strongly in nonviolence) traveled to London as representatives to the World Anti-Slavery Convention. When they tried to address the assembly, they and their British colleagues were not allowed to speak because they were female. Horrified at this blatant discrimination, Elizabeth and Lucretia were determined to organize a convention in the U.S.A. to champion the rights of women.

In 1848, the planned convention was finally held at Seneca Falls in New York. After much debate, the Seneca Falls Declaration demanded that women should have equal opportunities, fairer marriage laws, equal participation in the job market, and "*the sacred right to vote.*" The declaration also demanded the rights of citizenship—the right to work in politics and serve on juries.

A second convention was held in 1850 at Worcester, Massachusetts, and annually from then on. Around the country, like-minded women organized and agitated. During the American Civil War, Elizabeth Cady Stanton and Susan B. Anthony organized a national

SOURCE

STAMP

A centenary stamp celebrating the achievements of key figures in the Women's Movement in the hundred years after the Seneca Falls convention.

petition against slavery, and 400,000 names were collected. With the passing of the 13th Amendment, which included the words "*slavery … shall not exist within the United States,*" the debate turned to the giving of the vote to all freedmen. Many women thought that since color should not be a barrier to the vote, neither should gender. Elizabeth and Susan formed the American Equal Rights Association in 1866 and called for the 15th Amendment to include women as well as freedmen.

Many male politicians thought this was going too far and might damage the attempt to enfranchise men who had previously been slaves but were now free. When the 15th Amendment was passed in February 1869, it stated the *"vote shall not be denied ...on account of race, color, or previous servitude,"* but did not include gender.

Elizabeth and Susan responded immediately by forming a new organization, the National Women's Suffrage Association (NWSA), which with the help of their newspaper, *The Revolution*, campaigned against the 15th Amendment. A rival organization called the American Woman Suffrage Association (AWSA), run by Lucy Stone and her husband Henry Blacknell, was also founded in 1869. Not as radical as the NWSA, the AWSA defended the 15th Amendment because it enfranchised ex-slaves, and therefore, was a step in the right direction toward equality. Its members planned to win the vote for women on a state-by-state basis, which they believed was easier than trying to change the constitution.

In the election of November 1872, Susan tried a form of nonviolent direct action. She led a group of women to a polling station and demanded access. She was arrested and used her trial to gain maximum publicity. She told women to fight unjust laws *"that tax, fine, imprison, and hang women while they deny them the right of representation in the government."*

An illustration from 1875 shows a group of determined women trying to enter a New York polling station in order to vote.

Who could vote?

In Britain until the twentieth century, the vast majority of men qualified for the vote only if they owned or rented property. During the debates surrounding the Great Reform Act of 1832, Henry "Orator" Hunt tried to persuade Parliament to give the vote to unmarried women who met the property qualifications. Instead, when the Act became law, it actually referred to "male persons" so women were legally excluded from the franchise. The Reform Act increased the electorate in England and Wales from 435,000 to 652,000 by allowing a person who owned or rented a house with an annual value of £10 (about $1,200 today) in a town to vote.

Again in May 1867, when the Second Reform Bill was being debated, J. S. Mill tried to amend it by substituting "person" for "man," thereby allowing women to be included. His attempt was soundly beaten by 194 votes to 93.

Benjamin Disraeli's Second Reform Act more than doubled the electorate to over 2 million voters in the U.K. The new law enfranchised borough householders. This must have been very frustrating for the many women who would have qualified to vote as householders, but could only watch as many working men became enfranchised.

Lydia Becker decided to try and physically test the law. She contacted the women who qualified under

SOURCE

CARTOON

This cartoon gently pokes fun at J. S. Mill's attempts to include women in the 1867 Reform Act under the general term "persons."

MILL'S LOGIC, OR FRANCHISE FOR FEMALES
"Pray clear the way, there, for these—ah—persons."

the terms of the Act and told them to register to vote. Some were turned away, others actually registered. However, in November 1868, the courts ruled this as illegal.

Suffrage bills came and went every year during the 1870s without success. When J. S. Mill lost his seat in the 1868 election, Jacob Bright became the spokesperson in Parliament for women's suffrage. There was considerable confidence in 1884 that when the Liberal government's Third Reform Bill came before the house, an amendment could successfully enfranchise 100,000 well-off women. However, when the prime minister, William Gladstone, declared his opposition— *"I offer it the strongest opposition in my power"*—the amendment was defeated by 271 votes to 135. The Reform Act applied the property qualification of the boroughs to the counties, thus giving the vote to many agricultural laborers but still not to women.

This caused great resentment among many women, who as members of the middle and upper classes had to watch illiterate and poorly educated men get the vote, while they did not. This unfairness was felt strongly in the countryside, where there were 30,000 landowning female farmers who couldn't vote, yet the farm laborers employed by them could.

Interestingly, women were becoming more involved in politics as a result of

the Corrupt Practices Act of 1883. The government wanted to end corruption in elections so it imposed very strict limits on a candidate's expenditure at election time. As a result, political

Despite W. E. Gladstone's great liberal reforms—such as the establishment of a state education system—he stubbornly refused to consider giving women the vote.

parties became dependent on unpaid workers, and women volunteers in particular. Both the Women's Liberal Association (established in 1887) and the Conservative Party's Primrose League (established in 1883) had many thousands of members.

Why shouldn't women vote?

The "suffragists"—the name given to women who campaigned for the vote— used a whole range of arguments in their attempt to persuade the British public, politicians, and Parliament of their right to vote. The present system, they argued, was unjust and discriminatory. If a woman met the property qualification, her gender should not be an obstacle to her voting. If an unmarried, single, or widowed woman paid her taxes, contributing to the well-being of the country, she should be able to vote.

Many suffragists quoted the cry of the American colonists before they declared independence from Britain: "*No taxation without representation!*"

"Pit brow lasses" sitting on a stack of coal in 1912. Most were single and had no trade union to protect them. Many suffragists argued that with no one to look after women's interests, the vote was essential.

It seemed incredible to the suffragists that a woman who paid taxes could not elect those people who imposed the taxes. Also, women had no say in how their taxes were spent.

The suffragists also strongly believed that the vote was necessary to women's interests. They argued that men who were voters had their grievances listened to, discussed, and often acted upon. Women, who had no vote, were ignored and misunderstood. How, for example, was anything to be done about the very low wages of female workers, if women were excluded from the law-making process?

Helen Taylor, the stepdaughter of J. S. Mill, speaking to the London National Society for Women's Suffrage, touched on the physical ill-treatment of women by their husbands as an example of how women's interests and problems were being ignored. MPs were supposed to protect women, but she asked: "*…have any of these lawgivers brought in a bill for flogging men who ill-treat women? Not one.*"

Suffragists were very anxious to show how the vote would improve the quality of family life. If women became informed about politics and the outside world, it would make them better partners for their husbands and better educators of their children.

The vote would also strengthen public life. Women would raise levels of public service, contributing to and enriching the life of the nation in social matters such as education, health, and the treatment of the poor. Women participating in public life would be good for Britain's developing democracy.

Unsurprisingly, suffragists pointed out that in places where women had been given the vote, the experience had been a very positive one. The most famous example was the territory of Wyoming in 1869. Not only could women vote there, but they also served as Justices of the Peace. The town of Dayton, Wyoming, even had a woman mayor.

More impressively, suffragists listed legislation that women had been able to influence as a result of being enfranchised. Gambling had been declared illegal; women had rights to their own property; there were penalties for child neglect, abuse, and cruelty, and protection for children from tobacco and alcohol.

BOOK

Barbara Bodichon believed that female suffrage would promote: "*patriotism, a healthy, lively intelligent interest in everything which concerns the nation to which we belong.*"

Barbara Bodichon felt that giving the vote to women would be good for the nation and for democracy. She argued that giving the vote to women would bind the nation together.

Barbara Bodichon in *Before the Vote was Won: Arguments For and Against Women's Suffrage.*

Wyoming, known by suffragists as the "pioneer" state because it was the first to enfranchise women, has the words "equal rights" on its state seal.

11

Arguments against votes for women

From our point of view today, the arguments of suffragists look logical and persuasive. However, in the late nineteenth century, these ideas stood outside mainstream opinion. For many, both male and female, the idea of women's suffrage was dangerous, revolutionary, and unnatural.

Opponents often pointed out that women should not be able to vote because they could not fight for their country in wars. They believed that physical force was the basis of all political life and that women, because of their physical weakness and moral sensibilities against fighting, could not possibly contribute. As one MP said in 1873: "*All our history has been made by men and not by women; and our great empire, as it has been made, so must it be preserved …by the action of men.*" The message was clear—women should not involve themselves in areas of which they had no knowledge or experience.

Opponents of women's suffrage also claimed that the vast majority of women did not want the vote. The suffragist movement was portrayed as a tiny minority of noisy "fanatics." One MP boasted in 1872 that he had only met four women who wanted the vote so nothing should be changed.

In 1889, a well-known novelist, Mrs. Humphrey Ward, published *An Appeal Against the Extension of the Franchise to Women.* A granddaughter of Thomas Arnold, the famous principal of Rugby school in the U.K., she had inherited a strong sense of moral purpose. She believed in higher education for women, but not the vote. Mrs. Ward thought that giving the vote to women was "*distasteful to the great majority of women and mischievous both to themselves and the state.*" Furthermore, "*the pursuit of mere outward equality with men is for women, not only vain, but demoralizing.*" After its formation in July 1908, Mrs. Ward became a leading light in the Women's National Anti-Suffrage League (WNAL) and took part in public debates with suffragists at Cambridge University (U.K.). These

SOURCE

SPEECH

"*The mission of a working man's wife is to look after the home, to mind the baby, to cook the dinner, and do the washing. She has no time for electioneering.*"

Henry Labouchere, speaking in the House of Commons in 1904, outlines his views of the role of working class women.

were hot-tempered affairs, with students often heckling and shouting at her.

The WNAL attempted the same tactics as the suffragists by organizing a huge petition against women's suffrage, and in 1909, announced 250,000 signatures had been collected. By the summer of 1910, the League boasted 15,000 card-carrying members and there were branches all over the country. It was claimed the petition topped 320,000 signatures by 1911.

Despite all her active campaigning, Mrs. Ward continued to write novels, a number of which had anti-women's suffrage themes. In a letter to *The Times* in February 1909, she voiced the popular view among the antisuffragists that women were not skilled or experienced enough to be involved in politics. Britain's imperial affairs, with all its complexities and burdens, should "*be solved by the labors and special knowledge of men ... un-helped by the political inexperience of women.*"

Mrs. Humphrey Ward was a very popular novelist and tireless campaigner for the poor and destitute. However, her desire for reform did not include giving women the vote.

The NUWSS and Mrs. Fawcett

The 1880s and 1890s were a very frustrating time for suffrage campaigners in Britain. One of the problems was that the numerous suffrage societies often argued among themselves over the best campaigning methods. They also differed over whether all women should get the vote, or whether only single women were to be enfranchised. Were married women to be included? Should campaigners push for the same property qualification as men?

There was one major success for the suffrage movement in the 1890s. As far back as 1869, some women who paid property taxes could vote in local government elections. However, the 1894 Local Government Act meant that all women could vote in local government elections if they had the property qualification. They had to be the occupier (owner or tenant) of a house, apartment, or business premises worth at least £10 (about $1,300 today) a year. This Act stopped a lot of the arguing between groups, because now that many women could vote locally, it seemed more logical to push for the national vote.

By the late 1890s, there was a desire for unity within the movement, so in 1897, a National Union of Women's Suffrage Societies was formed (NUWSS). The organization was an alliance of the 17 largest suffrage societies in Britain and although its job was to organize activities and campaigns, it had no actual power over the individual groups. Its main strength was that it was not just centered on London but had great

SOURCE

PAMPHLET

This is the cover of an NUWSS pamphlet published in 1918. The cover illustrates that the NUWSS consisted of many different branches and has 449 societies united within it.

CHAIRMAN
M. ROBERTSON
SPEAKER
Mrs FAWCETT

10

NATIONAL UNION OF WOMEN'S SUFFRAGE SOCIETIES
PRESIDENT Mrs FAWCETT
LAW-ABIDING SUFFRAGIST

Mrs. Millicent Fawcett argues her case forcefully at a mass rally in London's Hyde Park. The banner clearly announces that the NUWSS worked within the law.

support throughout Britain. It was particularly strong in Lancashire among the female textile workers, so it was not exclusively middle class either.

In its early years, the NUWSS put pressure on Parliament and targeted MPs and candidates at election time, to find out if they were sympathetic to women's suffrage. Although the NUWSS was supposed to be a nonpolitical organization, it did have connections with the Liberal Party. Many people assumed that liberal values would include women's suffrage, so there was a great deal of optimism when the Liberal Party won a landslide election victory and formed a government in 1906. The NUWSS received another boost in 1907 when Mrs. Millicent Fawcett was elected as its

president. She was a great organizer and within two years, the NUWSS was employing ten national organizers and published its own newspaper, *Common Cause.*

One tactic the leadership introduced was the staging of mass processions or demonstrations. The first was held in February 1907 and was nicknamed the "Mud March," because 4,000 women had to walk through London in driving rain. This was quite daring for the time because it was not thought ladylike to take part in outdoor protests. To march required courage because if you were seen there, it might harm your reputation.

The struggle for suffrage in the U.S.A.

In the election of November 1872, Virginia Minor attempted to cast her vote in Missouri. As a result, she was arrested. Her case went all the way to the Supreme Court. Minor argued that the right to vote was part of her rights as a citizen, but the Supreme Court disagreed, saying the constitution did not allow women to vote. This ruling was important because the legal way to the vote had been blocked. Women would have to push for a federal

SOURCE

BOOK

"While poets and philosophers, statesmen and men of science are all … pointing to women as the new hope for the redemption of the race, shall the freest Government on earth be the first to establish an aristocracy based on sex alone … ? Was there ever made so base a proposition as 'manhood suffrage' in this American republic?"

Elizabeth Cady Stanton argued that America, "land of the free," must free half of its population.

Reference: Susan B. Anthony in *A History of Women's Suffrage*, 1869.

amendment in Congress and help individual states to introduce women's suffrage. In 1874, a Californian senator introduced a constitutional amendment that had been written by Susan B. Anthony. It declared that the right of "*citizens of the United States to vote shall not be denied …by the United States or any state on account of sex.*" During the debate, the senator for Delaware warned the amendment was a blow against God's laws and Christian marriage adding, "*You will no longer have that healthful and necessary subordinate of wife to husband …*" The amendment was defeated 76 votes to 6.

The two main suffrage groups, the NWSA and AWSA, joined together in 1890 under the name of the National American Woman Suffrage Association (NAWSA). Elizabeth Cady Stanton was president and Susan B. Anthony, vice president. Lucy Stone was chair of the executive committee. Lucy was in favor of concentrating on individual states winning the vote.

Wyoming had brought in full suffrage in 1869 but did not actually become a member of the Union until 1890. In 1893, Colorado granted full suffrage followed by Utah and Idaho in 1896. At this point, the momentum slowed and it would take 14 years until Washington granted full suffrage in 1910. In this period, the NAWSA pushed for and achieved referenda (when the whole electorate is asked to accept or reject a proposal) in only six states and lost every one. They had found themselves up against powerful corporations and brewing interests as well as strong political party machines. Brewers were against women's suffrage because many suffragist campaigners also supported temperance and wanted alcohol banned. Membership of the NAWSA fell to less than 100,000.

In 1889, when Wyoming was preparing its constitution for entry to the Union, the first clause was "*equal political rights for all male and female citizens.*" The constitution was sent to Congress for approval. Congress attempted to strike out the clause. The Wyoming Legislature responded with the words, "*We will remain out of the Union a hundred years rather than come in without women's suffrage.*" President Harrison signed the bill admitting Wyoming into the Union in June 1890. Wyoming was the first U.S. state to give women equal rights with men.

Suffragists on both sides of the Atlantic were skillful at spreading their ideas. In Ohio, it was believed to be useful to win men over to their cause.

Victories in New Zealand and Australia

While the suffrage movements in the U.S.A. and the U.K. were struggling in the 1890s, on the other side of the world dramatic victories were being won for women's rights.

There were no suffrage societies in New Zealand until 1885, when Mary Leavitt, representing the Women's Christian Temperance Union in the U.S.A. (WCTU), toured the country. At the end of the visit, 15 WCTU branches

had been set up and they attracted many well-educated and ambitious women who wanted to campaign for women's rights.

The WCTU began to campaign forcefully for the vote under its organizational director, Kate Sheppard. She encouraged members to lobby politicians who were sympathetic to women's suffrage. Three suffrage bills were sent to the Lower Chamber of Parliament in 1887, 1890, and 1891, but they all failed. Pressure continued with the new Franchise League formed

Women going to vote in Auckland, New Zealand. In the first election after women were enfranchised, 85% of qualified women voted, compared to only 69% of men.

in 1892. Petitions were arranged, large meetings organized, and pamphlets distributed. In 1893, a "monster petition" was sent to Parliament containing 31,871 signatures—including a quarter of all adult New Zealand women.

The Premier Richard Seddon did not support women's suffrage and tried to defeat the Electoral Bill (including women's suffrage) in 1893. Two members of the Upper House did not approve of Seddon's plans against women's suffrage and voted for the Bill instead of opposing it. In this way, all New Zealand's women—including Maori women—were enfranchised. In the next election held in the same year, 85 percent of women voted compared with only 69 percent of men. New Zealand became the first country to give suffrage to all women.

In Australia, it was to be the state of South Australia that would lead the way in women's suffrage. The democratic clubs, trade unions, and the WCTU (Mary Leavitt toured Australia in 1886) pushed for reform. One of its dynamic campaigners was Mary Lee, a trade unionist who founded the Women's Suffrage League.

On December 18, 1894, the Constitution Act Amendment Bill was passed by 31 votes to 14. All women in South Australia could vote. Western Australia followed in 1900.

When Australia united into a federation in 1902, South Australia

PAMPHLET

Mrs. Nellie Alma Martel was a member of the London and national committees of the Women's Social and Political Union in Britain. She had valuable experience of being a voter and of the Australian campaign. In 1906, The Women's Press published her pamphlet *The Women's Vote in Australia*. It ran to several editions before the outbreak of World War I.

said it would only join on the condition that all women were granted federal suffrage. In the constitution set up that year, federal suffrage was granted to all Australian women. Victoria was the last state to grant suffrage to women in 1908.

Both countries supported British suffragists sending over delegations to spread the word about the positive effects of female suffrage. At the height of the militant campaign in 1912, the Australian senate sent a resolution to the British government asking it to grant women the vote.

CHAPTER 4

The WSPU is formed

In October 1903, the veteran suffrage campaigner, Emmeline Pankhurst, founded the Women's Social and Political Union (WSPU) in Manchester, England, with her three daughters, Christabel, Sylvia, and Adela. Emmeline was particularly frustrated at the slow progress the suffrage movement had made and was critical of the NUWSS for "respectfully" asking for the vote. Emmeline believed there could be another way. The WSPU grew very slowly at first and by 1905, there were barely 30 members. However, the WSPU's slogan "Deeds Not Words" was to bring the organization a huge public profile.

Many bills went through the British Parliament between 1905 and 1913 to try to enfranchise women. They were either voted out or denied enough parliamentary time to be considered. In response, the WSPU decided to become more militant. In October 1905, Christabel and Annie Kenney attended a Liberal rally in Manchester to be addressed by Sir Edward Grey, a prominent member of the Liberal Party. To the surprise and shock of the audience, they interrupted the meeting and stood on their chairs and unfurled a Votes for Women banner. The meeting reacted angrily towards the women and they were forcefully ejected. Christabel wanted to get arrested so she kicked and spat at a policemen. She was sentenced to seven days in jail, and Annie Kenney to three days for refusing to pay their fines.

SOURCE

BADGES

Members of the WSPU wore these badges. The badge on the left was designed by Sylvia Pankhurst.

The story made the newspapers and within 16 months, the WSPU increased its membership to 47 branches. As an act of publicity the protest had been a success. Not long afterward, the *Daily Mail* mockingly called the women "suffragettes" and the name stuck.

In 1906, the WSPU set up its headquarters in London so it could exert pressure on MPs and ministers.

Two wealthy supporters—Emmeline and Frederick Pethwick-Lawrence—helped them. They took control of the finances and the supply of funds soon improved.

In the U.K., when a new government takes office, the monarch makes a speech to Parliament outlining its legislative program. When the new Liberal government's King's Speech in 1906 made no reference to women's suffrage, Emmeline Pankhurst was outraged. She led a march across London to Westminster where she attempted to hold a meeting outside Parliament. The police quickly dispersed the meeting. This was the first of the raids, or "rushes," Mrs. Pankhurst would make on Parliament.

The WSPU was unlike the other suffrage organizations in that Emmeline and Christabel ran it on dictatorial lines. They took all the major decisions and there was no democratic process allowing members to discuss or debate policy. This upset many supporters. Also, when it was formed, its early members were mainly working class. As the membership became more middle and upper class, it began to campaign for suffrage based on the property qualification. This disillusioned many of the original supporters. The slogan of "Votes for Women" was misleading, because with the new campaign, many working class women would not have got the vote.

The "monster meeting" on June 21, 1908, organized by the WSPU. The banner attacks Prime Minister Herbert Asquith and his refusal to grant "votes for women."

Constitutional methods

The women who campaigned under the NUWSS banner were called "suffragists" rather than "suffragettes" and used methods that were firmly within the law. Their peaceful and legal tactics were often borrowed from successful campaigns in the past. Many women had studied the Anti-Corn Law League's methods in the 1830s and 1840s, which had worked to repeal the protectionist Corn Laws. It had been a brilliantly successful campaign—the law was repealed in 1846—and involved meetings, demonstrations, propaganda, the pressuring of MPs, and the petitioning of Parliament. Above all, it was a single-issue organization. The NUWSS, who called themselves the "Law-Abiding Suffragists," were to use all these constitutional methods—unlike the suffragettes (the WSPU), who were prepared to break the law.

Meetings in the pre-radio, television, and computer age were extremely important. They were vital ways of gaining information, and the audience saw important or famous people "in the flesh." Some were quite

formal and took place in large central halls in big cities around Britain. They also took place outdoors at factory gates, in public squares, and in parks. Both the NUWSS and the WSPU held hundreds of these meetings during their campaigns.

SOURCE

POSTER

A clever poster produced by female artists who campaigned for women's suffrage. The contrast between deserving women and undeserving men is very clear. The poster was so popular that it was reproduced as a postcard.

They also held mass demonstrations. Not only was it good for the demonstrators to meet like-minded people, but it also fostered a spirit of camaraderie. When demonstrations were held in a big city, there was lots of publicity to promote the cause. In June 1908, there were two huge demonstrations in London. On June 13, the NUWSS marched with beautifully embroidered, home-made banners from the Embankment to the Royal Albert Hall in London. Speeches were made and songs were sung. On June 21, the WSPU marched in seven different columns and converged on Hyde Park, where 80 women speakers from 20 platforms addressed the crowd.

Written propaganda was an important way of spreading ideas, and most suffrage societies had a regular journal or weekly newspaper. The WSPU published *Votes for Women* from 1907, which was joined by the NUWSS' *Common Cause* in 1909. *The Suffragette*, edited by Christabel Pankhurst, appeared in 1913.

The newspapers all contained articles, poems, plays, and stories and often had amusing cartoons on the front. The bicycle was a very popular means of transportation in the early twentieth century and the societies exploited it. Suffragettes would

Poster for The Suffragette *newspaper, 1912. It shows Joan of Arc, the "patron saint" of the suffragette movement. Importantly, she is dressed for battle.*

decorate their bikes in WSPU colors— purple (for dignity), white (for purity), and green (for hope). The NUWSS organized bicycle pilgrimages to vacation resorts such as Brighton.

Both the NUWSS and the WSPU spent a lot of time and effort trying to win over MPs to their cause. There were always a number of MPs who were sympathetic to women's suffrage, and they could introduce Private Members Bills. Every year, bills to enfranchise women were proposed but they had no success.

Militant methods

In the period leading up to the Great War (World War I or WWI) in 1914, there was unrest in Britain. Industrial relations were poor and there were many violent strikes involving miners and transportation workers. When the Liberal government tried to give Ireland home rule (a limited form of independence), the Ulster Unionists rejected the measure and threatened rebellion if it went through.

The successes of the more violent protests were not lost on the suffragette (WSPU) leadership. They concluded that when men took a tough line and sometimes resorted to violence, they achieved results. Frustrated at the slow progress of the women's campaign and the fact that the new prime minister Herbert Asquith opposed votes for women, they decided to turn to violent methods.

In 1908, window smashing began. The prime minister's house at 10 Downing Street was attacked and the famous department store, Selfridges in Oxford Street, was targeted. Stones from the beach at Southend-on-Sea were brought up by train for the women to throw. Rich and well-to-do houses in the West End of London were favorite targets as were government departments such as the Home Office and the Treasury. Newspapers that were hostile to the

WSPU were attacked, especially the *Daily Mail* and *Daily News*.

On November 18, 1910, after a Conciliation Bill that would have enfranchised about a million women voters failed, there was an

SOURCE

DRAWING

This black-and-white drawing by Wilmot Lunt shows the suffragettes' window-smashing tactics.

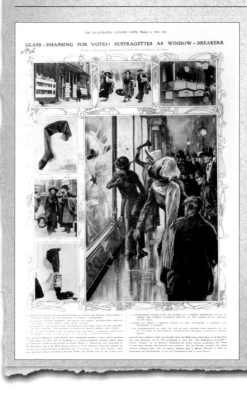

extraordinary pitched battle at the Houses of Parliament. On "Black Friday," as the suffragettes later called it, about 300 women tried to rush into the House of Commons. At first, the police did not arrest the women but threw them back into the arms of the crowd, which contained plain-clothes police officers. The women were treated very roughly, and a number of the protestors complained of indecent assaults by police. The battle raged all afternoon and by evening, 119 women had been arrested. When they appeared in court the next day, Winston Churchill, the Home Secretary, decided not to proceed with any prosecutions, and the women were released.

Emmeline Pankhurst's arrest on May 21, 1914. She had tried to enter Buckingham Palace to hand a petition to the king.

In 1911, the campaign was widened to include arson—the setting on fire of public buildings or private property. Mailboxes full of mail were set on fire as were railroad yards containing inflammable goods such as timber. Cricket pavilions were a favorite target because they were isolated and the preserve of men. Other male sports venues were targeted, such as soccer fields and grandstands at race courses. Golf courses were also attacked. Golfers sometimes found the words "No Vote, No Golf" scorched into the grass of the greens with acid. Fifty churches had been set on fire by 1914, because church authorities were accused of siding with the government.

One of the most infamous acts of the campaign happened on March 10, 1914, when Mary Richardson walked into the National Gallery in London and hacked Valesquez's painting entitled "Rokeby Venus" with an axe.

Alice Paul and the WSPU

In 1907, Alice Paul, a 20 year-old American student, came to study in Britain. A Quaker with a Master's degree from Pennsylvania University, she had won a scholarship to the Woodbrooke Quaker Study Centre in Birmingham. She also took social sciences classes at the University of Birmingham and during 1908–09 studied at the London School of Economics (LSE). She even found time to do social work in the poor areas of Birmingham and Dalston, in London.

Alice's life changed when she heard Christabel Pankhurst speak at a rally at Birmingham University. She was shocked to hear men in the audience shout her down with vicious verbal abuse. Although Christabel finished her speech, the other speakers could not, and the rally ended in chaos. Alice was impressed by the courage of the women to speak out for their beliefs despite the verbal and physical abuse. At once, she joined the WSPU and was a keen participant at weekly meetings. The lessons she would learn about women's suffrage campaigning in England would be very useful when she later returned to America.

In 1908, Alice found herself on the streets of London selling the newspaper *Votes for Women* with a friend from LSE, Rachel Barrett. They had to stand in the gutter to avoid arrest for obstructing the pavement. Obscenities were shouted at them, and local workers often showered them with rotten fruit and vegetables.

The first time Alice was arrested was in Bermondsey, south London, in 1909 when protesting against the prominent Liberal cabinet minister, David Lloyd

Women selling **The Vote** *newspaper of the Women's Freedom League, a splinter group from the WSPU. The League disapproved of violence, but many of its members were imprisoned for refusing to pay their taxes.*

George. Alice hated public speaking so arrest and placement in the cells was less frightening to her than making a speech.

When she joined a march led by Emmeline Pankhurst to see Herbert Asquith, the prime minister, she met another American student and WSPU member, Lucy Burns, who would be her friend in the movement for many years. The march was broken up, and the protestors were arrested and herded into police vans.

In 1909, Alice and Lucy were chosen by Emmeline to be her assistants and they traveled to Scotland, helping to organize events and local offices. At Berwick-on-Tweed in northern England, they interrupted a speech by Sir Edward Grey, the foreign secretary. When Grey outlined his government's policy Alice leapt up and shouted "*Well, these are wonderful ideas but couldn't you extend them to women?*" She was promptly arrested.

A more serious episode happened on November 9, 1909, when Alice and Amelia Brown disguised themselves as cleaners, hid in the Guild Hall in London, and waited for the Lord Mayor's banquet. When Prime Minister Asquith rose to speak, Amelia broke a pane of glass with her shoe and both women shouted "*Votes for Women!*" They were sentenced to a month's hard labor for refusing to pay the fines and damages. Once in prison, Alice went on hunger strike, but was force-fed twice a day for a month. It was a terrible ordeal and when she left prison on December 9, 1909, she was gravely ill.

Alice Paul, a skillful campaigner, learned all about the importance of the media and publicity while working with the Pankhursts in Britain.

27

Alice Paul returns to the U.S.A.

It took Alice Paul a long time to recover from the hunger strike and the force-feeding, and in January 1910, she decided to leave the U.K. and return home to the U.S.A. On January 20, she arrived in New York to be met by a crowd of reporters and photographers bombarding her with questions. She was famous!

Alice had learned a great deal in Britain about protesting and she volunteered to run a committee on street meetings. In September 1911, she organized a meeting in

Independence Square, Pennsylvania, where over 2,000 people listened to 18 speakers, including Alice, who was conquering her fear of speaking in public.

In December 1912, she moved to Washington, DC, to work for NAWSA in pushing for a federal suffrage amendment of the constitution. On March 3, 1913, as chair of the Congressional Committee, Alice organized the first suffragist parade in the capital, just before Woodrow Wilson's inauguration as president. Alice had learned a great deal from the Pankhursts and as a result, the parade was brilliantly organized, even down to the colors of the marchers.

The parade of March 3, 1913, was a triumph for Alice Paul. Referring to American history, one of the banners used Abraham Lincoln's famous quote: "No Country Can Exist Half Slave and Half Free."

The procession contained 26 floats, 10 bands, four mounted brigades, and 8,000 marchers.

At the centerpiece, a float, followed by a marching band, proclaimed: "*We demand an amendment to the constitution of the United States enfranchising the women of this country.*" Unfortunately, trouble began when some spectators started insulting the marchers and members of the crowd were pushed into the procession. The police did very little to contain this violence, and as a result, 200 people had to go to the hospital. Alice was convinced that the police and city officials had deliberately tried to break up the parade. The event gained a lot of publicity but not all of it was welcome. NAWSA's leadership was unimpressed with what they thought were Alice's militant and confrontational tactics.

In the end, Alice left NAWSA and set up the Congressional Union in 1914. She blamed the Democratic Party for being responsible for the delay in granting women's suffrage. As a result, her Union campaigned against Democratic candidates in elections if they did not support votes for women. This caused outrage for many in NAWSA who regarded the Democrats as their main supporters.

Undeterred, in January 1917, Alice and her new National Women's Party (NWP) started round-the-clock picketing of the White House in an attempt to pressure President Wilson.

SOURCE

PLACARD

In 1917, the "Silent Sentinels" stood outside the gates of the White House in Washington with banners of accusing questions aimed at the president.

Women, known as "Silent Sentinels," stood like statues and held posters full of accusing statements and questions such as "*Mr. President, how long must women wait for liberty?*" Many who were arrested and imprisoned went on hunger strikes. The public were sympathetic and this helped the women get early releases.

Alice Paul has been compared to Christabel Pankhurst. However, being a Quaker, she was devoted to nonviolence and her clever campaigns played a major role in gaining women's suffrage in the U.S.A. in 1920.

The hunger strikes

In June 1909, the WSPU in Britain decided to petition King Edward VII. They believed they could legally do this under the Bill of Rights of 1689. A suffragette walked into the Houses of Parliament and began painting the walls with Clause V of the Bill: "*It is the right of the subject to petition the King, and all commitments and prosecutions for such petitioning are illegal.*" Her name was Marion Dunlop Wallace and she was promptly arrested. Refusing to pay a £5 (around $600 today) fine, Marion was sentenced to a month in prison.

When she arrived at Holloway prison, London, she refused to change into prison uniform or to be examined. She demanded "first division" treatment—political prisoner status.

Political prisoners could wear their own clothes and receive food packages. When this was refused, she informed the prison guards she was going on a hunger strike. Nearly four days later and in a very weak state, Marion was released.

This was the first time the hunger strike had been used as a political weapon, and the WSPU adopted it as official policy for prisoners. Not only did it generate massive publicity for the cause, but the authorities released prisoners when they became very sick.

In September 1909, news leaked out of Winson Green Prison, Birmingham, that suffragette prisoners on hunger strikes were being force-fed. The decision was taken for two reasons: the government clearly did not want any of the suffragettes to die and

THE CAT AND MOUSE ACT
PASSED BY THE LIBERAL GOVERNMENT

THE LIBERAL CAT
ELECTORS VOTE AGAINST HIM!
KEEP THE LIBERAL OUT!

'THE SUFFRAGETTE' PRICE 1d

SOURCE

POSTER

This political poster captures the violence of the Liberal government's policies toward the suffragettes. It calls on voters to keep the "Liberal Cat" out of government.

become martyrs to their cause; also, they wanted to keep the women in prison for as long as possible. About 1,000 prisoners were force-fed liquid food through the nostrils or mouth by rubber tubes that often weren't even sterile.

A powerful propaganda poster showing a reconstruction of the government's policy of force-feeding. This is referred to as "torturing women."

This caused an outrage in many circles, and gradually, public opinion turned against the government and its "barbaric" methods. Councils all over the country passed resolutions in favor of the women's demands and sent them to the government.

Perhaps fearing that someone would die and cause damaging publicity, the government decided to act. In 1913, it passed the Temporary Discharge for Ill-health Act, which was immediately dubbed the "Cat and Mouse" Act by the suffragettes. If prisoners, by their actions, were in danger from ill-health, they were released until they recovered and then re-arrested. It was used many times against Emmeline Pankhurst. Some suffragettes chose to go into hiding, which is why the authorities secretly photographed them in prison to help the police track them down later.

This tactic was also used in the U.S.A. during 1917. After the arrest of the NWP pickets outside the White House in October (see page 29), a number of suffragists went on hunger strikes, including Alice Paul and Rose Winslow. Fourteen other women started hunger strikes, too. After 22 days during which she was force-fed, Alice and most of her colleagues were released by the authorities.

SOURCE

JOURNAL

"Prisoners were held down by force, flung on the floor, tied to chair and iron bedsteads … while the tube was forced up the nostrils … The wardress endeavored [tried] to make the prisoner open her mouth by sawing the edge of the cup along the gums … the broken edge caused … severe pain. Food in the lung of one prisoner … caused severe choking, vomiting … persistent coughing. She was hurriedly released … suffering from pneumonia …"

Doctors expressed their concern about force-feeding women prisoners in the *British Medical Journal*, 1912.

Fighters for the cause

One fighter for the vote was the suffragette martyr, Emily Davison. She had been a brilliant scholar and achieved a first-class honors degree from the University of London. Emily joined the WSPU in 1906 and quickly became an active member. She was arrested and imprisoned four times in 1909 and in September, went on a hunger strike in prison.

After her release, she was arrested again in Newcastle for throwing stones at Lloyd George's car. Emily was sentenced to one month's hard labor at Strangeways Prison, Manchester. Again, she went on a hunger strike, but the prison authorities decided to force-feed her. To prevent this, Emily barricaded herself in her cell. She was hosed with water. The guards burst in and carried her out, freezing cold and weak, and revived her in a hot bath. They then force-fed her.

Emily sued the prison authorities and was awarded £2 (around $250 today) in damages. She continued her

NEWSPAPER

A shocking newspaper photograph of the moment Emily Davison brought down the king's horse in the Derby in 1913.

campaign, setting mailboxes on fire in 1911. Arrested and imprisoned, she went on a hunger strike again.

On June 4, 1913, on Derby Day at Epsom, Emily waited for the king's horse to come around Tattenham Corner. WSPU member Mary Richardson saw her that afternoon and recalled: *"Suddenly, she slipped under the rail and ran out into the middle of the race course."* She died of her injuries. The suffragettes had their first martyr.

Another influential fighter for the cause of women's suffrage was Lucy Burns. She had met Alice Paul in 1909 while they were both active in the WSPU in Britain (see page 27) and was a remarkable woman. Her main claim to fame, apart from having fought two suffrage campaigns in different countries, was to be the most imprisoned suffragist in the U.S.A.

Lucy returned to the U.S.A. from Britain and set up the first suffrage headquarters in Washington, DC, in January 1913. She helped Alice to organize the huge parade in March 1913. Lucy was an inspirational leader during the White House picketing of 1917. She led most of the picket demonstrators and paid a heavy price. She was sentenced to six separate spells in prison between June 1917 and January 1919. This was on top of the four prison terms she served in Britain.

Her worst experience was undoubtedly at the notorious Occuquan workhouse in Virginia during November 1917. She smuggled out an account of her ordeal on tiny scraps of paper. The workhouse prison regime was brutal. Denied political prisoner status, Lucy went on a hunger strike. On the seventh day, weak and very sick, she was force-fed. When she refused to open her mouth, the prison doctor pushed a tube up her left nostril. The pain in her nose and throat was intense and her nose bled heavily. The food dumped into her stomach felt *"like a ball of lead."*

SOURCE

SLOGAN

"Resistance to tyranny is obedience to God."

This was the slogan on the paper that wrapped the stones thrown at Lloyd George's car by Emily Davison.

Lucy was seen as a leader of the women and was removed by the police to the local jail with another hunger striker, Dora Lewis. There they refused to work or wear prison clothing and were locked in separate cells.

An inspiration to a whole generation of suffragists, Lucy retired from political campaigning after women gained the vote in 1920.

Reactions to the war

When Britain declared war on Germany on August 4, 1914, the WSPU leadership immediately called off its militant campaign and threw its weight behind the war effort. Christabel returned from exile in France where she had fled in 1912 to escape arrest. Emmeline called for the conscription of men into the armed forces and for women to take their places in the arms factories.

For the NUWSS, it was not so simple. Many of the national officers were against the war and this led to a split over whether to support the war effort or not. Some of the national officers left, with the exception of Mrs. Millicent Fawcett and her treasurer, and formed the Women's International League for Peace and Freedom. Both groups suspended their suffrage campaigns during the war, and although Mrs. Fawcett appealed for peace just before the declaration of war, once fighting started, she appealed to her membership (echoing the famous Kitchener recruitment poster) *"Women, your country needs you."* She believed that a German victory would destroy democracy, but was never as vehemently anti-German as Emmeline and Christabel Pankhurst.

The WSPU quickly got to work with the government, in an effort to recruit women war workers. By 1915, the group was in close contact with Lloyd George, the Minister for Munitions, whose department financed "The Great Procession of Women" in July. The event was to encourage women to join the labor force and had the slogan "a woman's right to serve." It was brilliantly organized, like WSPU marches in the past. Instead of the suffragette colors, Emmeline wore red, white, and blue. Lloyd George had clearly forgiven the WSPU for bombing his new home in 1913. To prove its loyalty to the war effort, the WSPU newspaper *The Suffragette* was re-named *Britannia*.

The war concreted the rift in the Pankhurst family that had started before the war. Sylvia Pankhurst had formed her East London Federation of Suffragettes, which Emmeline, her mother, and Christabel, her sister, did not approve of.

Sylvia's belief in supporting the cause for working-class women was disliked by Emmeline and Christabel and when war broke out, Sylvia proclaimed herself an "antiwar agitator." Working closely with the local Labor Party, she set up nurseries, toy factories, cheap restaurants, and free milk and health centers for the poor in London's East End.

Mrs. Fawcett's position was probably the most difficult. She knew that if the NUWSS was seen to be pacifist by the government and general public, this could be damaging to the suffrage cause after the war. Throughout the war, she constantly stressed that Britain's use of force was for justice and every woman should do all she could to save the country from German militarism. When a peace conference was held in neutral Holland in April 1915, the NUWSS did not allow any of its societies to attend, for Mrs. Fawcett said that talk of peace was "*akin to treason.*"

Leaders of the Women's Movement applauded the government's "Register of Women for War Service" set up in 1915. Any woman could sign up at her local Labor Exchange and gain access to a large variety of job vacancies.

SOURCE

POSTER

This striking poster encouraged women to enter the factories and to make munitions for the war effort. The grateful soldier in the background is waving his approval of women doing their part.

THESE WOMEN ARE DOING THEIR BIT

LEARN TO MAKE MUNITIONS

The home front and the front line

One of the main arguments used both in Britain and the United States by antisuffrage campaigners was that women could never contribute to the defense of the nation (see page 12). The Great War proved this to be totally wrong. Women leapt at the opportunities the war gave them. With hundreds of thousands of men volunteering to fight, women were

A young munitions worker welds in an arms factory in 1915. Women very quickly picked up industrial skills that were thought to be the preserve of men.

ideally placed to take over their jobs. Many ended up in occupations they could only have dreamed of before the war. They became bus drivers, window cleaners, chimney sweeps, farm workers, firefighters, electricians, and factory and shipyard workers.

Many women saw the war as an opportunity to leave the drudgery of domestic service. It is thought that the number of servants dropped by about 400,000 during the war and many never returned. In fact, the postwar, British middle-class complaint: "You can't get the servants today" dates from this time. Many women were eager to earn good money in the munitions factories (they were called "munitionettes") and leave the endless tasks of cleaning fire grates and dirty kitchens behind. Women were also needed in engineering factories and soon became skilled with lathes and micrometers (instruments for making measurements). Male workers grudgingly accepted them in their factories, and trade union membership among women increased to over one million.

The munitions factories were not without their dangers. The chemicals the women handled were often toxic and many became sick and some even died. In the largest munitions factory, the Woolwich Arsenal, many women suffered from stomach cramps, sickness, and constipation working with the explosive TNT. The risks from explosion were considerable and despite strict rules governing clothing, accidents did take place. Dreadful explosions took place in Silvertown in east London in 1917 and Chilwell near Nottingham in 1918, killing many workers including women.

Some women served close to the front lines in Europe. There was a huge demand for nurses and ambulance drivers, and many women answered the call. They saw the realities of the conflict at close quarters, and many young women saw the horrors of the first mechanized war. The VADs (Voluntary Aid Detachment) was a popular destination for many middle- and upper-class women, and although many were based in Britain, some worked in hospitals in France, Belgium, and Italy. Women who enlisted in the First Aid Nursing Yeomanry experienced the dangers of front-line fighting and had to be equipped with gas masks.

SOURCE

QUOTE

"… the magnificent contribution, which the women of the United Kingdom have made to … our country's cause."

In 1916, even the "old enemy," Herbert Asquith, admitted to Mrs. Fawcett how much he appreciated women's participation in the war. Would it bring them the vote?

Early in 1917, recruitment for the Women's Army Auxiliary Corps began. Known affectionately as WAACs, the corps was founded to send uniformed women to France and Belgium to carry out nonmilitary duties, such as those of clerks, cooks, and map artists.

Mairi Chisholm and Elsie Knocker driving their ambulance through the ruins of northern Belgium. They manned a first-aid post near the front line for most of the war.

The vote at last!

In 1916, the British government set up a Speaker's Conference consisting of MPs to report on women's suffrage. It soon became clear that any radical proposal, such as universal suffrage (votes for all over the age of 21), would lead to the complete rejection of women's enfranchisement. The conference then considered raising the age at which women could vote. It was thought that it would be better to give the vote to married women, who would probably be mothers, rather than abandon the vote altogether. This older group was believed to be more deserving of the vote than younger factory workers, because they had given husbands and sons to fight in the army and navy.

In January 1917, the conference voted by 15 votes to 6 to support the idea of women's suffrage. They left Parliament to decide whether 30 or 35 should be the voting age. When it announced its findings, a lot of suffrage groups were angry that although all 21-year-old men could vote (19 if they had been in the armed forces), women would have to be in their 30s.

Just because women's suffrage was included in the Speaker's report, it did not necessarily mean Parliament would agree with its findings. Mrs. Fawcett,

the experienced campaigner, busily lobbied ministers all through the early months of 1917 along with members of other suffrage groups.

Prime Minister Lloyd George, at the head of a new coalition government, promised that a bill including votes for women would be introduced. He stressed that it was a Commons bill rather than a government bill and that

SOURCE

QUOTE

"There are a great many evils which I hope to see remedied now that women have secured the vote. The problem of women's employment, both industrial and professional, is one, which demands immediate attention. … while I am delighted with the vote, I am by no means satisfied. A law which gives a boy the vote and withholds it from a woman until she is thirty cannot be said to be a fair one."

Mrs. Fawcett, head of the NUWSS, pointed out that there were still more struggles to be won for equal rights.

National News, March 10, 1918.

It is all smiles as a young mother brings her family with her to vote in the December 1918 general election.

MPs would vote according to their consciences. The NUWSS was quick to put pressure on all supporting MPs not to miss the vote.

The great day came on June 19, 1917. The Representation of the People Bill (with the women's suffrage clause) was passed by a huge majority of 385 votes to 55. This majority was extremely important because the Lords would be much less likely to vote against such a popular measure.

As it turned out, the Lords clearly did not want a dispute with the Commons and they passed it by 134 to 71.

So, after many years of struggle, the Representation of the People Act became law on February 6, 1918, and finally gave the vote to women. They did not automatically get the vote at the age of 30. They had to be occupiers or the wives of occupiers, and as a result, 22 percent of women 30 or over could not vote. Mrs. Fawcett admitted the act was a "motherhood vote," because 83 percent of the women who could vote were wives and mothers.

The Act had enfranchised 8,400,000 women. It was not a complete victory because equal suffrage had not been won. However, in February 1918, there was much celebration for what was, for many, a very sweet victory.

Victory in the U.S.A.

Anna Shaw became the president of NAWSA in 1904 and put a lot of energy into state referenda to gain women's suffrage in as many states as possible. A victory was scored in 1910 when Washington voted for full suffrage. Over the next few years, the NAWSA gave publicity to the progressive laws that Washington state began making: an 8-hour working day for women; a minimum wage for women; free kindergartens; and the abolition of the death penalty. More states followed suit: California in 1911; Kansas, Oregon, and Arizona in 1912; Alaska in 1913; and Montana and Nevada in 1914.

A real breakthrough came in 1915 when Carrie Chapman Catt became President of NAWSA. Carrie was a superb organizer and very cleverly did not ally the NAWSA too closely with either the Republican or Democratic parties. Carrie came up with the so-called "Winning Plan." NAWSA's money and resources were allocated to each state according to how likely it was to pass a state constitutional amendment. The more states that did this, the more pressure would be put on the federal government and the president in Washington, DC.

Carrie was afraid that Alice Paul's NWP's campaigns, especially after the picketing of the White House in 1917, would turn President Wilson against their cause. This is why NAWSA had to be seen to be working within the law— a similar attitude to Mrs. Fawcett's NUWSS in Britain.

Suffragists patriotically celebrating the passing of the 19th Amendment in August 1920.

The turning point came when the U.S.A. entered World War I in April 1917. Suffragists reacted to war in different ways. Some formed peace societies and campaigned for pacifist solutions, such as the American Union Against Militarism. Others, notably the NAWSA, threw their weight behind the war effort as an expression of their patriotism. Alice, being a Quaker and committed to nonviolence (pacifism), continued with the picketing campaign rather than backing the war effort. It is interesting that Emmeline Pankhurst, with whom Alice had campaigned in Britain, suggested that the NWP should follow the WSPU example and suspend all suffrage campaigns during the war.

One very strong argument that the suffrage movement used well was the fact that the U.S.A. had joined Britain and France in a war "for democracy against autocracy" (Germany and Austro-Hungary being autocracies). How could any country claim to be democratic, yet not allow its women to vote in elections?

President Wilson came around to this point of view. In September 1918, he appeared in front of the Senate and announced that amending the constitution in favor of women was important for the winning of the war. In 1919, the 19th Amendment was sent to all the states of the Union for ratification.

It took 15 months, including a thrilling two-vote victory in the last

SOURCE

LETTER

"Hurrah. And vote for suffrage and don't keep them in doubt. I notice some of the speakers against. They were very bitter. ... Don't forget to be a good boy and help Mrs. Catt put 'Rat' in Ratification."

This was the letter in 24-year-old Harry Burn's pocket that his suffragist mother had written to him. Harry's final vote in the Tennessee chamber gave women the vote by 49 votes to 47 in 1919.

Extract from *Baltimore Sun*, September 5, 1920.

state to vote, Tennessee. On August 26, 1920, the 19th amendment, also called the "Anthony Amendment" after Susan B. Anthony's attempt in 1874, was added to the constitution.

Alice Paul unfurls a banner at the National Women's Party Headquarters. Each star represents a state that had passed the 19th Amendment giving women the vote. Here, they had just heard that Tennessee had ratified.

Why did it take so long to get the vote?

In the United States, the women's suffrage movement dated from the 1840s and in Britain it gained momentum in the 1860s. Women secured equal suffrage in 1920 in the U.S.A. but not until 1928 in Britain. Why was the campaign to win the vote such a long and drawn-out affair?

The simple fact is that for many years, most men did not want women to have the vote. The society that

SOURCE

POSTCARD

An antisuffrage postcard suggesting that women were active politically only because they could not find a husband or a partner.

developed in Britain and the U.S.A. during the nineteenth century was overwhelmingly male-dominated. Men controlled the economy, the law, education, and the employment market. Women had no access to these areas, and it was expected they would be dependent on men. Women were seen as weak and vulnerable and men were supposed to protect them.

The female world was seen as the home, the private sphere. Women's talents were domestic, and not in the public sphere of work or politics. A good example of how this idea was reinforced was in Britain in 1878. The new board (state) schools had to teach domestic science—washing, cooking, cleaning, and sewing—to all girls. The message was clear. Young women were being prepared for the home and not for work.

From many men's point of view, males were in control and anything that tried to upset this status quo was revolutionary. When suffragists demanded the vote, many men saw this as dangerous and even threatening. Sadly for the suffragists, many women agreed with these men that they should not be on equal footing with men. In Illinois in 1897, antisuffragists stated *"We believe that men are ordained to govern in all forceful and material matters, because they are men." Ordained* means "God-given."

We have seen how "forceful" men were in protecting their interests. When women marched at the British Houses of Parliament in 1910 (later known as Black Friday, see page 25), the response was brutal.

According to medical witnesses, many women received black eyes, bloody noses, dislocations, cuts, and bruises. In the U.S.A., during 1917, when the White House pickets were

arrested, a group of women prisoners were subjected to a "Night of Terror" in the Occuquan Workhouse in Virginia. Guards armed with guns and clubs severely brutalized—both verbally and physically—the female prisoners, even Mary Nolan from Florida, who was 73.

A suffragette wrestles with a policeman during the Black Friday demonstration, November 18, 1910. This was probably the most violent confrontation of the suffragette campaign.

Another important factor in the struggle was that opponents of the suffragists attacked their gender rather than the rationale of their ideas. They were subjected to vicious stereotyping. Suffragists and especially suffragettes were called "warped old maids," "destroyers of the family," "marriage rejects," or even worse.

The reason the struggle took so long was because many men were not willing to give up their positions of power and influence without a fight.

Movement for equality

In Britain, the women's suffrage movement did not stop just because of the 1918 Act. It pushed on to win equal suffrage with men at the age of 21. In 1918, the NUWSS became the National Union of Societies for Equal Citizenship (NUSEC), and Mrs. Fawcett was replaced by Eleanor Rathbone as president. However, it was not the powerful, vibrant force it had been before the war—membership

Eleanor Rathbone runs as an independent candidate for East Toxteth, Liverpool, in the general election of 1922. She was not elected, but ran again successfully in 1929.

had dropped dramatically from 447 affiliated societies to 234. Also, the NUSEC was no longer a single-issue organization. Eleanor Rathbone was also interested in the New Feminism agenda, which aimed for access to contraception (birth control) and family allowances, as well as equal suffrage. New groups such as Lady Rhondda's Six Point Group kept up the pressure for equal suffrage.

Some of the old tactics were deployed again. On July 3, 1926, with the help of Emmeline Pankhurst, Lady Rhondda organized a mass rally in Hyde Park in which 3,000 women called for the vote at the age of 21.

The prime minister of the day, Stanley Baldwin, was a firm believer in equal suffrage and won over his Conservative Party. The Representation of the People (Equal Franchise) Act became law in 1928. One important result was that women were now in the majority—52.7 percent of the electorate were women. Five and a half million more women gained the vote. The struggle for equal suffrage was over, but the new struggles over women's pay and employment rights were just beginning.

TIMELINE

1792	Mary Wollstonecraft's *A Vindication of the Rights of Women* published.
1825	William Thompson and Anne Wheeler's *Appeal of One Half of the Human Race* published.
1832	The Great Reform Bill. Henry "Orator" Hunt tries to include the vote for propertied unmarried women.
1848	Women's Convention held at Seneca Falls, New York.
1866	Petition for the enfranchisement of women organized in Britain.
1867	John Stuart Mill unsuccessfully presents the petition to Parliament during the debate of the Second Reform Bill.
1869	Suffrage granted to women in Wyoming.
1869	The 15th Amendment passed, granting the vote irrespective of "race, color, or previous servitude," but not to women.
1884	The Third Reform Bill in Britain does not include women.
1890	NAWSA formed in the U.S.A.
1893	Suffrage granted to women in New Zealand.
1897	The NUWSS formed in Britain. Mrs. Fawcett is president.
1902	The Commonwealth of Australia technically grants votes to all women. The last state to introduce it in Australia was Victoria in 1908.

1903	The WSPU formed by the Pankhursts.
1905	The WSPU begins its militant campaign.
1909	First hunger strikes by WSPU prisoners. Force-feeding is introduced.
1912	The WSPU's mass window-smashing campaign begins.
1913	Emily Davison dies after injuries sustained on Derby Day.
1914	Mary Richardson slashes *Rokeby Venus* with an axe in the National Gallery, London.
1914	The Great War (World War I) begins. All militancy is suspended by the suffragettes for the duration of the war.
1914	Alice Paul sets up the Congressional Union in the U.S.A.
1917	Alice Paul forms the National Women's Party (NWP) and begins picketing the White House. Some arrested NWP women begin hunger strikes.
1918	The Representation of the People Bill becomes law. Most women over 30 in Britain can vote.
1920	The 19th Amendment becomes law in the U.S.A., giving all women the vote.
1928	The Representation of the People (Equal Franchise) Act allows women in Britain over 21 to vote.

GLOSSARY

Autocracy
Rule by one person, usually an emperor.

Coalition
A temporary union of political parties that forms a government.

Constitution
A written statement outlining the basic laws and principles by which a country or organization is governed.

Corruption
Doing something dishonestly and often being paid money for it.

Discrimination
Being treated differently or worse because of race, color, or gender.

Enfranchise
To give the right to vote in elections.

Federal
Relating to a form of government in which power is divided between one central and several regional governments.

Feminism
The movement that supports women having the same civil rights as men and equal opportunities.

Franchise
The right to vote in elections.

Freedmen
Slaves who had been liberated after the American Civil War.

Heckling
To interrupt a public speaker (often aggressively).

Inauguration
When a person, such as a president, takes office.

Legislative
Describes the writing and passing of laws.

Martyr
Someone who dies for their cause.

Militant
Prepared to take direct action, which might involve arrest, in support of a cause.

MP
A Member of Parliament in the government of Great Britain.

Petition
An appeal to an authority, signed by many people.

Picketing
The act of standing outside a building to protest about something.

Pit brow lasses
The girls and women who toiled above ground at the coal mines.

Property qualification
The rule that meant you had to own property or land to qualify to vote.

Protectionist
To protect home-produced goods from the competition of foreign imports.

Quaker
A member of a Christian sect that is peaceful and does not believe in using violence.

Radical
A person who challenges accepted ideas about politics, the economy, or social issues.

Ratepayers
People who pay local taxes according to the value of their property.

Ratification
The act of giving official approval to a formal document such as a law or treaty.

Referendum (plural: referenda)
A vote taken by the whole of the electorate on a single issue.

Repeal
To officially withdraw a law.

Senator
An elected or appointed member of the senate (law-making body of the government) of the United States.

Sterile
Free from germs and absolutely clean.

Suffrage
The right to vote in elections.

Suffragette
A campaigner for giving the vote to women. A suffragette was prepared to break the law using force or violent methods to obtain the vote.

Suffragist
A campaigner for giving the vote to women. Suffragists used legal or constitutional methods to obtain the vote.

Temperance
To abstain from drinking alcohol.

Toxic
A substance that is poisonous.

Trade union
An organization for workers that protects their pay and conditions.

Treason
Plotting against or harming one's own country.

FURTHER INFORMATION AND WEB SITES

FURTHER READING

History Firsthand: Women's Suffrage by Richard Haesly (Greenhaven Press, 2002)

Industrial America: Great Women of the Suffrage Movement by Meachen Rau (Compass Point Books, 2006)

People at the Centre of: Women's Suffrage by Deborah Kops (Blackbirch Press 2003)

WEB SITES

Due to the changing nature of Internet links, Rosen Publishing has developed an online list of Web Sites related to the subject of this book. This site is regularly updated. Please use this link to access this list: http://www.rosenlinks.com/doc/suff

INDEX

Numbers in **bold** refer to illustrations.